W9-CBQ-556

ART DECO

RICHARD STRINER

ABBEVILLE
STYLEBOOKS™

AN ARCHETYPE PRESS BOOK

ABBEVILLE PRESS · PUBLISHERS

NEW YORK · LONDON · PARIS

CONTENTS

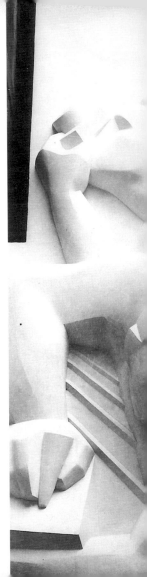

INTRODUCTION

No style has been more neglected, undervalued, misunderstood, or camped up. —Ada Louise Huxtable, *New York Times*, 1974

What is Art Deco—and is it proper to call it a style? Historians do not agree. The most accurate way to think about Art Deco—a term coined in the 1960s in honor of the 1925 Exposition Internationale des Arts Décoratifs et Industriels Modernes in Paris—is to view it as a cluster of design trends that expressed certain powerful moods of the 1920s, 1930s, and 1940s. Its repertoire was derived from sources as diverse as classical antiquity and futuristic fantasy. It used exotic ornamentation while assimilating streamlined industrial design. It interacted with—and it infiltrated—a great many other design modes, and the result was often a welter of exotic hybrids.

Yet for all the diversity of elements that found their way into Art Deco, and for all the challenge of trying to define the essence of the movement, many people think that they know the thing when they see it—at least in its boldest examples—and they know it as a spirited expression of the years between the world wars. Walk up New York's Lexington Avenue and gaze at the silvery spire of the Chrysler Building: one can feel the rhythms of the Jazz Age. One can *feel* the messages of power, technology, exotica, and elegance shimmering down from the ziggurat atop the skyline.

Throughout the world the design legacy of Art Deco conveys the spirit of the interwar decades. A rounded corner, or a zigzag terrace, or an ornamental panel with exuberant sunbursts, flamingos, or gazelles: even those whose knowledge of the period is casual can correctly place such designs within this era.

The 1920s and 1930s were years of tremendous controversy in design. A bitter war was raging between apostles of radical modernism and defenders of design traditions. The most militant radicals argued that design ought to be cool, austere, and abstract—devoid of any references to previous centuries, devoid of any ornamentation. Defenders of tradition were indignant at the radicals' aggressiveness. They were utterly determined to maintain design continuity. And here is where the nature of Art Deco becomes clear—for in the course of this war among designers and architects, Art Deco sought mediation and compromise. Along with its other attributes, Art Deco became a middle range between conservative and radical design.

The imagery of Art Deco was broadly inclusive. It was drawn from the ancient past—classical features from ancient Greece and Rome as well as from Egypt. It was drawn from the distant future—with images from the world of Buck Rogers. And it was drawn from contemporary views of the 1920s, 1930s, and 1940s—twentieth-century visions of machines, jazz, and speed. All were combined in a broad and captivating movement.

In Art Deco the most divergent and sometimes hostile tendencies were synthesized and combined. The combinations were often uneasy ones—but this is the source of the energy and tension that have stimulated Art Deco devotees for more than a half century.

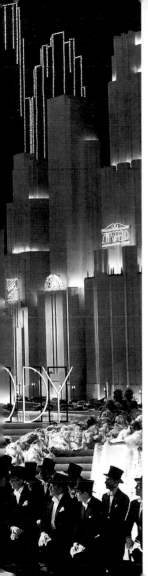

THE JAZZ AGE

The Jazz Age—the Age of the Machine—the Aspirin Age—the Streamlined Age—the Depression Era—the Bitter Years—the Age of Swing: the years between World War I and World War II saw turbulent moods, but amid changes and confusion some thought that they could glimpse the dawn of a new day.

Eleanor Powell, dressed in top hat and tails, was the picture of interwar elegance in the film *Broadway Melody of 1938*. The backdrop of New York skyscrapers helped feed the public frenzy for these symbols of progress.

The 1920s, 1930s, and 1940s were years of extraordinary turbulence, achievement, and disaster. Booms were juxtaposed with depressions. Visions of elegance and hopes for a streamlined future coexisted with apocalyptic fears: of another war, of revolutions or economic ruin—even of the decline and fall of Western civilization. Heroic statesmanship vied with political cowardice, and public moods were a giddy alternation of euphoria, terror, myopia—and endurance.

Woodrow Wilson had hoped that America's entry into World War I could transform that struggle into a "war to end war." But the victors proved incapable of building an architecture of peace. America turned to an interlude of drift. European politics festered: Germany faced recurrent crises, Italy became Fascist, and Russia passed from the age of Lenin to the age of Stalin.

Artists in the 1920s struggled to express the spirit of the age—or to repudiate it. Modernist visions of utopian order emerged from the Bauhaus in Germany and the pens of architect-oracles such as Le Corbusier. Others condemned technological progress as a snare and a delusion: T. S. Eliot descanted morbidly on the "waste land" of modern life.

Architecture or [R]evolution. Revolution can be avoided.
—Le Corbusier, *Towards a New Architecture,* 1923

Charles Lindbergh's 1927 flight to Paris in his *Spirit of St. Louis* captured the imagination of people on both sides of the Atlantic.

The stripped-down, "liberated" look of this French woman in the 1920s—the scanty bathing attire would have been a scandal in earlier decades—helped pave the way for the stripped-down, streamline aesthetics of the 1930s.

Already, we can glimpse the community of tomorrow as a place unified and harmonious . . . coordinated, artist-determined, machine-realized.
—Sheldon and Martha Cheney, *Art and the Machine*, 1936

Life was thrilling for a great many people in the 1920s: this was the age of jazz, of radio, of "crazy rhythm," of the freedom to go "runnin' wild." But the 1930s were a very different decade. A worldwide depression was especially severe in the United States: when Franklin D. Roosevelt took the oath as president in 1933, America's manufacturing output had dropped to almost half its 1929 level and almost a third of America's work force was unemployed. In the same year that FDR's New Deal began, Adolf Hitler took over in Germany. The armies of Imperial Japan were already on the march in Manchuria.

Paradoxically, the grimness of the 1930s was accompanied by elegance and hope. In popular music, the rhythms of the 1920s evolved into the up-beat, sensuous lilt of 1930s "swing." Many people in America viewed the New Deal as a matchless opportunity for twentieth-century pioneering. Concurrent with New Deal public works projects—the Tennessee Valley Authority, for instance—industrial designers created a vogue for exuberant streamlining. Almost everything from toasters to locomotives took on a crisp new appearance that broadcast progress through technology.

1914 1915 1916 1917 1918 1919 1920 1921 1922 1923 1924 1925 1926 1927 1928 1929

POLITICS & SOCIETY

■ Panama Canal opens
■ WWI begins
■ U.S. enters WWI
■ Russian Revolution
■ Flu epidemic strikes
■ Versailles peace treaty
■ Prohibition starts in U.S.

Lindbergh flies to Paris ■
Sacco and Vanzetti executed ■
Henry Ford produces the Model A ■
Stock market crashes ■

■ Mussolini takes power in Italy
■ Lenin and Wilson die
■ *Mein Kampf* (Hitler)

LITERATURE & PERFORMING ARTS

Ulysses (Joyce) ■
This Side of Paradise (Fitzgerald) ■
The Waste Land (Eliot) ■
Babbitt (Lewis) ■
Decline of the West (Spengler) ■
Rhapsody in Blue (Gershwin) ■
Charleston dance craze ■
The Great Gatsby (Fitzgerald) ■
The New Yorker magazine ■
Metropolis (Lang) ■

Sound films begin with ■
Al Jolson's *The Jazz Singer*
An American in Paris (Gershwin) ■
A Farewell to Arms (Hemingway) ■
The Sound and the Fury (Faulkner) ■

VISUAL ARTS & DESIGN

Bauhaus founded in Weimar ■
Dadaist exhibition, Berlin ■
Vers une Architecture (Le Corbusier) ■
Exposition Internationale des Arts Décoratifs ■
et Industriels Modernes, Paris
Bauhaus relocated to Dessau ■
Barclay-Vesey Building (Walker) ■
Bullock's Wilshire (Parkinson) ■
The Metropolis of Tomorrow (Ferriss) ■
Chanin Building (Sloan and Robertson) ■

1914 1915 1916 1917 1918 1919 1920 1921 1922 1923 1924 1925 1926 1927 1928 1929

1930 1931 1932 1933 1934 1935 1936 1937 1938 1939 1940 1941 1942 1943 1944 1945

POLITICS & SOCIETY

■ Japan invades Manchuria ■ Spanish Civil War begins   WWII ends ■

■ Franklin Roosevelt elected ■ Germany's *Hindenburg* explodes

■ Earhart solos across the Atlantic ■ Hitler annexes Austria

■ Hitler becomes chancellor ■ Kristallnacht pogrom against German Jews

■ New Deal launched ■ Germany invades Poland; WWII begins

■ Hitler purges Nazi rivals ■ Nazi Blitzkrieg; conquest of France

■ Mussolini invades Ethiopia ■ Battle of Britain

■ Huey Long assassinated ■ Roosevelt reelected to third term

■ Roosevelt reelected ■ Nazis invade Soviet Union

■ Hitler occupies Rhineland ■ Japan attacks Pearl Harbor

LITERATURE & PERFORMING ARTS

■ *Brave New World* (Huxley)

■ *Autobiography of Alice B. Toklas* (Stein)

■ *Flying Down to Rio* (Astaire-Rogers)

■ Benny Goodman's Palomar Ballroom concert

■ *Porgy and Bess* (Gershwin)

■ *U.S.A.* (Dos Passos)

■ *The Wizard of Oz*

■ *Gone with the Wind*

■ *The Grapes of Wrath* (Steinbeck)

■ *Mr. Smith Goes to Washington*

VISUAL ARTS & DESIGN

■ Chrysler Building (Van Alen) ■ Johnson Wax Administration Building (Wright)

■ Empire State Building
(Shreve, Lamb and Harmon) ■ Golden Gate Bridge (Strauss)

■ International Style exhibition,
Museum of Modern Art ■ New York World's Fair

■ Golden Gate Exposition, San Francisco

■ Radio City Music Hall (Deskey)

■ Century of Progress Exposition, Chicago

■ Bauhaus closed by Nazis

■ Machine Art exhibition, Museum of Modern Art

■ Rockefeller Center (Hood et al.)

■ Fallingwater (Wright)

1930 1931 1932 1933 1934 1935 1936 1937 1938 1939 1940 1941 1942 1943 1944 1945

PRODUITS DE BEAUTE
PARFUMS FARDS

COIFFURE POUR DAMES

SALON DE COIFFURE

LINA CAVALIERI

SALON DE COIFFURE
ONDULATIONS PERMANENTES
SOINS DE BEAUTE
MANUCURE
PEDICURE CHINOIS

The short-skirted, flat-chested, cloche-hatted "flapper" of the 1920s became an important new symbol of reckless freedom, but by the early 1930s hemlines had fallen, bobbed hair was replaced by "Marcel" waves—perhaps with a platinum bleach job in emulation of Jean Harlow—and cloches gave way to berets, half-turbans, and sloping headgear with brims. Smart tailored suits by day might yield to slinky bias-cut gowns in the evening. By the early 1940s hemlines were rising again but hairstyles were highly variable: upswept hairdos vied with shoulder-length cuts held in place with snoods and even long and silken tresses like Veronica Lake's. Teenage girls pranced in saddle shoes.

Men's fashions departed less from prewar conventions. Many signature items—"eight-piece" caps and brown-and-white wingtip shoes—were carryovers. Trousers were fuller, waistlines were high, and ties were accordingly short. Double-breasted suits were popular. Flannels and tweeds were the mode, finished off by a fedora. The man-about-town emulated Fred Astaire or the Prince of Wales, but by the early 1940s the exaggerated zoot suit was a fad among hip teenage boys who caught the fever of jive culture.

In the 1920s the latest Parisian attire was worn by patrons of Lina Cavalieri's beauty salon (opposite) and displayed on sleek store racks (above).

In their sophisticated clothes and elegant settings (pages 16–17), actors in films such as *Our Modern Maidens* (1929) helped bring Art Deco's allure to the silver screen.

An important Art Deco painter in France was the Polish émigré Tamara de Lempicka, whose Jazz Age portraiture achieved international fame. Her *Self-Portrait (Tamara in the Green Bugatti)* dates from 1925.

Amid the modernisms that were struggling for artistic influence between the wars—from Cubism to Surrealism—certain artists were affected strongly by Art Deco. Among the most prominent was Jean Dupas, known for *The Parakeets* at the 1925 Paris exposition and murals for the ocean liner *Normandie.*

Art Deco also influenced (and was influenced by) graphic artists and illustrators, notably Russian émigré Erté (fashion illustrations), A. M. Cassandre (poster design), Rockwell Kent and Lynd Ward (woodcut book illustrations), Miguel de Covarrubias (stylized caricatures), Hugh Ferriss (moody architectural renderings), and George Petty (streamlined, airbrushed ads and pinup girls).

Art Deco was even more prominent in the work of sculptors: Paul Manship (the golden *Prometheus* at Rockefeller Center), Lee Lawrie (Rockefeller Center's monumental *Atlas),* Carl Paul Jennewein (Justice Department), and Oskar J.W. Hansen (Hoover Dam). Others applied their skills to architectural ornamentation: Edgar Brandt helped define the spirit of the 1925 Paris exposition and pioneered the Art Deco repertoire with jazzy juxtapositions of floral motifs, frozen fountains, and geometric forms.

Notable Posters

Normandie (1925,
   A. M. Cassandre)

Maurice Chevalier
   (1925, Charles Kiffer)

Shell Series (1930s,
   E. McKnight Kauffer)

Berlin Olympics (1936,
   Ludwig Hohlwein)

DECO STYLE

Some of the greatest landmarks of the twentieth century emerged from the Art Deco era—treasures such as the Palais Stoclet in Brussels, the Théatre des Champs Elysées in Paris, Broadcasting House in London, the Chrysler and Empire State buildings, Rockefeller Center, the Golden Gate Bridge, and Hoover Dam. Beyond the realm of superlative monuments, a wealth of vernacular structures spread the look and feel of Art Deco around the world.

The frozen fountain motif atop the Porte d'Honneur (Henri Favier and André Ventre) at the 1925 Paris exposition became a worldwide symbol of Art Deco.

ZIGZAGS, ZIGGURATS, AND STREAMLINES

Despite the diverse origins of Art Deco, a number of features were recurrent: the synthesis of classical symmetry and modernist simplification of form; zigzag terracing and projecting ziggurats on buildings; design symbolism that suggested both the ancient past and the distant future; an ornamental repertoire of simple motifs such as sunbursts, fountains, and leaping gazelles; the combination of new machine-age materials with far more traditional ones; and, by the early 1930s, the pervasive appearance of curvilinear streamlining.

In a great deal of Art Deco architecture, the massing of the building itself was its ornament: zigzag terracing and streamlined contours were sculptural, expressive devices. Yet both of them affected not only the massing of the buildings but also the ornamental details, such as zigzag corbelling of brickwork and the tell-tale symbolic speed stripes that were often applied to both streamlined furnishings and streamlined buildings of the period.

From Hollywood sets to kitchen appliances, from airplanes to grocery packaging, Art Deco became one of the most important visual signatures of its age.

In his study for the maximum mass permitted by New York's 1916 zoning law, architectural renderer Hugh Ferriss captured the powerfully expressive qualities of Art Deco's setback terracing.

These terraced crags, these soaring towers and pylons and piers overwhelm. . . . This is at once a new Babel and a City Divine.
—Sheldon Cheney,
The New World Architecture, 1930

This poster for the Paris exposition was designed by Robert Bonfils.

Art Deco's forebears included Art Nouveau and the Vienna Secession. One of the masterpieces by Austrian modernist Josef Hoffmann— a residence in Brussels called the Palais Stoclet—displayed prototypical Art Deco elements even in 1905.

Well before the Paris exposition of 1925, the tendencies that made up Art Deco had begun to coalesce. As early as the 1910s German architect Erich Mendelsohn was starting to develop architectural streamlining. The work of Eliel Saarinen and Bertram Grosvenor Goodhue synthesized classicism with modernist simplification of form. But it was the Paris exposition that catalyzed Art Deco.

In New York, skyscraper architects began to assimilate Art Deco rapidly. From the Barclay-Vesey Building (1925, Ralph T. Walker) to the Chrysler Building (1930, William Van Alen), Empire State Building (1931, Shreve, Lamb and Harmon), and Rockefeller Center (1935, Raymond Hood and Associated Architects), New York emerged as an international proving ground for Art Deco. In dozens of other cities spectacular Deco buildings were under way by the late 1920s.

At the same time Art Deco began to take on the streamline aesthetic. Promoted by industrial designers such as Raymond Loewy, Norman Bel Geddes, Walter Dorwin Teague, and Henry Dreyfuss, it was initially an aerodynamic treatment for vehicles. But streamlining was also chosen for a range of stationary objects, not the least of them buildings.

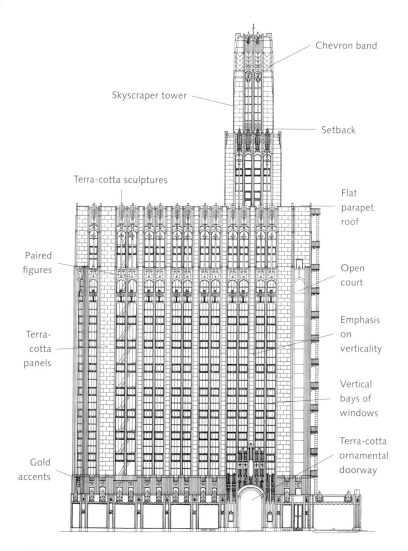

Chevron band

Skyscraper tower

Setback

Terra-cotta sculptures

Flat parapet roof

Paired figures

Open court

Terra-cotta panels

Emphasis on verticality

Vertical bays of windows

Terra-cotta ornamental doorway

Gold accents

DECO STYLE

ART DECO FEATURES

Setbacks: Stepped or setback tapering of skyscrapers (necessitated by some zoning restrictions), embodying the ziggurat iconography common in Art Deco.

Towers: The overall form of some tall Deco buildings and a crowning element on others.

Ornamentation: A repertoire typically including rectilinear motifs in low relief, in the form of zigzags, bands of chevrons, straight lines, and some curvilinear patterns.

Razed in 1969, Los Angeles's Richfield Building (1930, Morgan, Walls and Clements) was one of Art Deco's greatest losses.

Materials: Exterior cladding relying on smooth materials from concrete to limestone, with veneers and accents in terra cotta, aluminum, or stone.

Colors: Polychromatic effects in pale and subdued pastels or bold combinations such as black and gold.

Roofs: Predominantly flat, including terraces in ziggurat-shaped buildings; dramatic spires on some skyscrapers.

Parapets: Low, protective and decorative wall extensions placed along roof edges, often as a site for projecting elements to heighten a building's verticality.

Windows: Composed in vertical bays or horizontal bands with occasional ornamental windows in geometric shapes, such as portholes; expansive display windows at ground level to accommodate stores and retail facilities in large commercial structures.

Doors: Dramatic and imposing doorways or entrances to major buildings, sometimes surrounded by elaborate ornamentation.

Sculpture: Integrated ornamental sculpture, usually in the form of low-relief stone panels or spandrels featuring allegorical figures, sometimes in contrasting colors and textures.

ARCHITECTS

**Walter Ahlschlager
(1887–1965)**
Netherland Plaza Hotel,
Cincinnati (1930)

**William S. Arrasmith
(1898–1965)**
Greyhound bus terminals
(1930s)

**Paul Philippe Cret
(1876–1945)**
Folger Shakespeare Library,
Washington, D.C. (1932)

John Eberson (1875–1954)
Art Deco movie theaters
(1920s–1930s)

Henri Favier
Porte d'Honneur,
Paris exposition (with André
Ventre) (1925)

**Bertram Grosvenor Goodhue
(1869–1924)**
Nebraska State Capitol,
Omaha (1932)

Josef Hoffmann (1870–1956)
Palais Stoclet, Brussels
(1905–11)

Henry Hohauser (1896–1963)
Hotels, Miami Beach (1930s)

Raymond Hood (1881–1934)
Daily News Building,
New York (1931);
McGraw-Hill Building,
New York (1931);
Rockefeller Center (with
Associated Architects),
New York (1935)

Ely Jacques Kahn (1884–1972)
Film Center Building,
New York (1928)

Thomas Lamb (1871–1942)
Art Deco movie theaters and
bus stations

**Robert Mallet-Stevens
(1886–1945)**
Pavilion of Tourism,
Paris exposition (1925)

Pierre Patout (1879–1965)
Monumental Concorde Gate,
Paris exposition (1925)

Timothy Pflueger (1892–1946)
Paramount Theater,
Oakland, Calif. (1930)

Eliel Saarinen (1873–1950)
Saarinen House,
Cranbrook, Detroit (1929)

Henri Sauvage (1873–1932)
Primavera Pavilion,
Printemps Department Store,
Paris exposition (1925)

**Gilbert Stanley Underwood
(1890–1960)**
Wilshire Tower,
Los Angeles (1928);
Union Station, Omaha (1929)

Joseph Urban (1872–1933)
New School for Social
Research, New York (1929)

**William Van Alen
(1883–1954)**
Chrysler Building,
New York (1930)

André Ventre (1874–1951)
Porte d'Honneur,
Paris exposition (with Henri
Favier) (1925)

Ralph T. Walker (1889–1973)
Barclay-Vesey Building,
New York (1925)

ARCHITECTURE FIRMS

Austin Company
Streamlined commercial and
industrial buildings (1930s)

Delano and Aldrich
Pan American Seaplane Base,
Miami (1932)

Fellheimer and Wagner
Union Terminal,
Cincinnati (1933)

**Graham, Anderson, Probst
and White**
30th Street Station
and Suburban Station,
Philadelphia (1929)

Holabird and Root
Board of Trade, Chicago (1928)

Morgan, Walls and Clements
Richfield Building,
Los Angeles (1930);
Thomas Jefferson High School,
Los Angeles (1936)

John and Donald Parkinson
Bullock's Wilshire Department
Store, Los Angeles (1928)

Schultze and Weaver
Waldorf-Astoria,
New York (1931)

Shreve, Lamb and Harmon
Empire State Building,
New York (1931)

Sloan and Robertson
Chanin Building,
New York (1929)

Wallis, Gilbert and Partners
Hoover Factory, London (1935)

INDUSTRIAL DESIGNERS

Norman Bel Geddes (1893–1958)
Horizons (1932)

Donald Deskey (1894–1989)
Radio City Music Hall,
New York (1932)

Henry Dreyfuss (1904–72)
Democracity, New York's
World's Fair (1939)

Raymond Loewy (1893–1986)
Studebaker (1930s);
planes, trains, trucks, ships,
automobiles

Walter Dorwin Teague (1883–1960)
Bluebird Radio (1937–40)

Russel Wright (1904–76)
Home furnishings

SCULPTORS

Carl Paul Jennewein (1890–1978)
Sculpture, Justice Department,
Washington, D.C. (1934)

Lee Lawrie (1877–1963)
Atlas, Rockefeller Center,
New York (1935);
Sculpture, Nebraska State
Capitol, Omaha (1932)

Paul Manship (1885–1966)
Prometheus, Rockefeller
Center, New York (1935)

Hildreth Meiere (1892–1961)
Medallions, Rockefeller Center,
New York (1935)

ARTISANS

Edgar Brandt (1880–1960)
Metalwork,
Paris exposition (1925);
Cheney Brothers Store,
New York (1925)

René Paul Chambellan (1893–1955)
Gates, Chanin Building,
New York (1929)

Jean Dunand (1877–1942)
Smoking room,
French Embassy,
Paris exposition (1925)

Paul T. Frankl (1887–1958)
Furniture designs

René Lalique (1860–1945)
Glass designs

Jean Puiforcat (1897–1945)
Silver designs

Emile-Jacques Ruhlmann (1879–1933)
Furniture designs

Louis Süe and André Mare (Süe et Mare)
Furniture designs

Walter von Nessen (1889–n.a.)
Lighting

Sidney Waugh (1904–68)
Steuben Glass designs (1930s)

Kem Weber (1889–1963)
Furniture, interior,
and set designs

ARTISTS & ILLUSTRATORS

Robert Bonfils (1886–1971)
Posters and bookbinding

A. M. Cassandre (1901–68)
Posters

Miguel de Covarrubias (1905–57)
Caricatures

Tamara de Lempicka (1898–1980)
Adam and Eve (1932)

Jean Dupas (1882–1964)
The Parakeets (1925);
Murals, S.S. *Normandie* (1935)

Erté (1892–1990)
Magazine and fashion
illustrations

Hugh Ferriss (1889–1962)
Architectural illustrations

Rockwell Kent (1882–1971)
Book illustrations

Jean-Emile Laboureur (1877–1943)
Engravings

Georges Lepape (1887–1971)
Magazine illustrations
and prints

Louis Lozowick (1892–1973)
Art, stage sets, store windows

John Vassos (1898–1985)
Book and stage designs

Some thought that San Francisco's Golden Gate Bridge (1937, Joseph B. Strauss) would "mar if not utterly destroy the natural charm of the harbor famed throughout the world." Instead, it was one of the most impressive—and beloved—engineering feats of the new machine age.

The Golden Gate Bridge

Length: 8,900 feet

Span: 4,200 feet

Towers: 746 feet high

Cables: 36 inches in diameter

Load: 160 million pounds

Roadway: 200 feet high

By the 1920s steel-frame construction had long since permitted structures taller than many would have dared to imagine before, but architects, planners, and critics remained divided on how they should be designed. Cities were expanding outward as well—and again, divergent theories developed about the forms (and limits) of urban and suburban expansion. Closely linked was the car and the welter of challenges it presented.

In their search for solutions to these problems, designers enjoyed the best of industrial technology and new materials. Reinforced, prefabricated, and monolithic concrete construction added to the architectural repertoire. Air conditioning initiated a gradual but profound transformation in a whole way of life. Industrial glass block and pigmented structural glass (Carrara glass and Vitrolite) offered options both exotic and futuristic.

The Owens-Illinois Building at the 1933 Century of Progress Exposition in Chicago fueled a craze for hollow glass blocks that profoundly affected Art Deco design. Pigmented structural glass also became a mania in the 1930s, especially to streamline older storefronts—a fad encouraged by the glass companies' "Modernize Main Street" campaigns.

O U T S I D E

In the mid-1920s novelist and critic Rebecca West observed that on New York's Lexington Avenue "there is a vast apartment house which rears its dark masses like the pyramids and which like them is an example of mystery-making in stone." Unlike the cool sublimity of Bauhaus modern architecture, Art Deco buildings became sources of swanky enchantment—of Jazz Age whimsy and delight.

Miami Beach's Century Hotel (1939) was designed
by the prolific local architect Henry Hohauser.
In tropical buildings, stucco tended to predominate,
along with regional materials such as keystone,
a porous rock containing fossils.

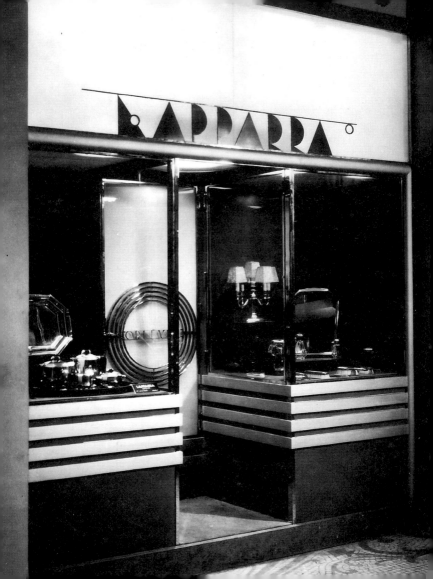

MATERIALS AND COLORS

When it comes to Deco building materials and colors, generalizations can be risky: for every rule there were exceptions. Many public and commercial buildings, for instance, were clad in restrained and dignified materials like limestone and granite, but the Richfield Building (1930) in Los Angeles shone with black and gold terra-cotta tiling. Other Art Deco structures were adorned in similarly bold materials. Favorites for commercial buildings such as gasoline and bus stations included new materials like porcelain enamel. Aluminum, stainless steel, and similar metals were used for trim and decorative panels. Other architectural ornamentation included terra cotta, glass block, Carrara glass, cast concrete, concrete mosaic, limestone, and "art stone" (artificial stone).

The Art Deco color palette varied widely, although certain preferences can be discerned in particular locales (pastels in Miami Beach) and building types (rich and bright colors in movie theater interiors). Designers frequently resorted to polychromatic compositions. Many of them could shift from the most restrained and muted colors to outrageously bold sensuality, depending on client, location, and purpose.

The most up-to-date materials were often applied to Art Deco storefronts, such as the entrance to the shop of Lapparra, a Parisian silver merchant—reached by a mosaic sidewalk.

Monumental sculpture, color, and metallic finishes— gold, silver and platinum—are all part of the so-called "moderne." That terra cotta is the only material in which all three effects may be combined is obvious.
— National Terra Cotta Society, 1930

Octagonal portholes added geometric detailing to the Essex House (1938, Henry Hohauser) in Miami Beach.

Edgar Brandt's wrought-iron doors for the 1925 Cheney Brothers Store in New York feature a spectacular frozen fountain in gilt bronze. Art Deco nature symbols often had a simplified form and a hard, machinelike edge.

Art Deco doors and entrances could be extremely ornate and elaborate: the entrance provided an obvious showplace for Art Deco's theatricality. At the Circle Tower Building in Indianapolis (1930, Rubush and Hunter), bronze doors are topped by patterns of Egyptian figures, all of which in turn were surrounded by a limestone arch bearing intricate floral ornamentation. Otherwise unremarkable houses sometimes sported Art Deco entrances.

Art Deco windows often emphasized the verticality or horizontality of a building's overall mass. Especially in low-rise, streamlined buildings, horizontal window banding was used as a compositional device of great importance. Some Art Deco buildings had stained-glass windows, and variant window shapes—portholes, for instance, and triangular sunray windows like the ones in the Chrysler Building's spire—were used to accentuate a building's ornament. In some cases window walls of glass block achieved a purpose that was functional—illumination with no loss of privacy—and ornamental.

ENTERTAINMENT

The Cincinnati Music Hall (1879, Samuel Hannaford) was an elaborate High Victorian Gothic example of the opera house. Every small town coveted its own little version of such a structure.

From traveling shows and circuses to operas and oratorios, the Gothic Revival era offered a kaleidoscope of entertainment activities. Museums brought scientific curiosities and fine art to many, often in impressive Gothic structures, such as the old Boston Museum of Fine Arts (1878, John Sturgis) and Frank Furness's Pennsylvania Academy of the Fine Arts (1876), a Venetian Gothic confection. At Brighton,

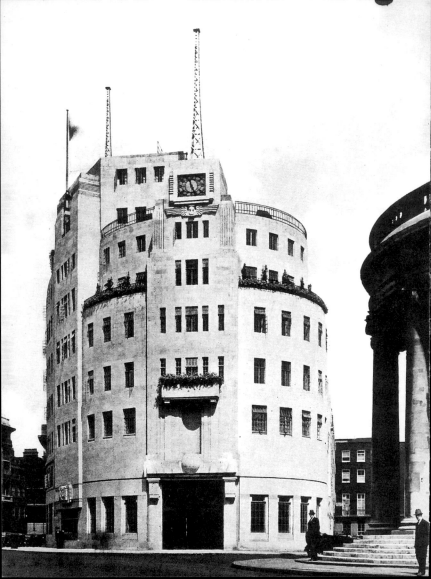

ROOFS AND PORCHES

For the most part, gabled roofs were infrequent in buildings where Art Deco was in evidence. Flat roofs tended to predominate, either in absolute terms—as in the streamlined hotels of Miami Beach—or as the tops of terraces in buildings configured like ziggurats. This setback treatment in some cases stemmed from municipal regulation: many zoning ordinances by the mid-1920s required that the upper stories of tall buildings be narrowed by terracing to "tame" the visual effect of their bulk and mass. The result was a dramatically sculpted appearance almost made to order for Art Deco. In the case of some skyscraper towers, although by no means all, the crowning treatment was a melodramatic spire that pushed the building's height skyward.

Porches or vestiges of porches were found in some Deco buildings. Full-fledged porte-cochères appeared in a number of apartments, hotels, and department stores—such as Bullock's Wilshire (1928) in Los Angeles and the Sedgwick Gardens apartments in Washington, D.C. (1931, Mihran Mesrobian). Dramatic marquees appeared in hundreds of Art Deco theaters, apartment houses, offices, and stores.

London became a laboratory for innovative Art Deco designs. The BBC made a virtue of necessity with its Broadcasting House (1932, G. Val Myer). Deco curves fit well into a tight, oddly shaped lot, and transmission towers added the needed touch of verticality to its setback cylinder of a building.

Every roof [in 1939] will be a garden. …Houses, in all climates, will have flat roofs. Every floor will have more terraces.
—Norman Bel Geddes, *Ladies' Home Journal,* 1931

ORNAMENT

The bronze gates of
the W. P. Story Building
(1934, Morgan,
Walls and Clements)
in Los Angeles present
a wealth of stylized
faces, sun rays, floral
motifs, and abstract
geometric forms.

Art Deco ornamentation derived to a great
extent from four overlapping categories: abstract geometric forms, nature motifs, machine symbols, and allegorical depictions.
The overlap could be interesting. A zigzag
pattern could represent a nature symbol—
the thunderbolt—along with the electric
flash of broadcasting; a sunburst could also
suggest a machine part such as a gear.

Sculpture (often bas-relief panels) depicted pseudo-mythic heroes or divinities:
personifications of elemental forces (like
power) inspirited in modern technology.
Overtly classical references sometimes were
mixed with allegorical figures of a timeless
sort: the sculptures *Prometheus* and *Atlas* in
Rockefeller Center (1935) were juxtaposed
with the figure *Wisdom*, a Jehovah-like presence soaring fifty-five feet above the entrance
to the RCA Building, and with medallions depicting Dance and Song.

On the Selig Commercial Building (1931,
Arthur E. Harvey), also
in Los Angeles, black
and gold terra cotta
outlines a decorative
frieze of chevrons and
floral motifs.

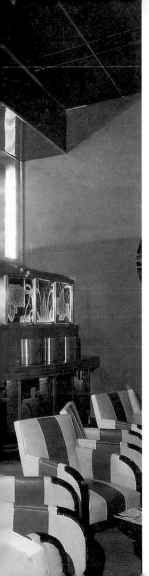

In F. Scott Fitzgerald's *Tender Is the Night*, Dick Diver and Rosemary Hoyt set foot in a modernistic Paris salon. "The effect was unlike any part of the Decorative Arts Exhibition—for there were people in it, not in front of it. Rosemary had the detached false-and-exalted feeling of being on a set...." However "false and exalted" Deco interiors seemed at first, in time a multitude of people probably felt exalted and at home in them.

This extraordinary Art Deco bar was added to the Carlton Hotel in Washington, D.C., in the 1930s. The bartender was hidden inside.

45

A stairwell of glass block surrounded a sweeping modernistic stairway in the Bruning residence (1936, George Fred Keck) in Wilmette, Illinois.

[Architects] build at a given time, using all the devices, ideas, and materials and needs of that time, and what comes out is the result of such thinking.
—George Fred Keck

Critic Lewis Mumford observed that the lobby and corridors of New York's Barclay-Vesey Building (1925), with its intricate floral "seed catalogue" ornamentation, looked like a "village street in a strawberry festival." Art Deco walls—and sometimes ceilings—ranged from floral to geometric and from extremely simple to extremely opulent. Intricate plasterwork, woodwork, murals, Carrara glass, mirrored glass, glass block, and textiles all were molded to designers' imaginations. Stairways ascended with graceful and stylized metalwork railings.

Three interiors epitomize the exuberant end of the spectrum. The Oakland Paramount Theater (1930) is still resplendent with intricate plaster, metal, glass, and textiles. Donald Deskey's interior for Radio City Music Hall (1932) features a lobby mural by Ezra Winter, carpets and wallpapers by Ruth Reeves, and materials from aluminum to pony hide, suede, and white kid. In Cincinnati's Union Terminal (1933) were mosaic murals by Winold Reiss above marble wainscoting; paneling in the director's office depicted the terminal itself in wood inlays; and the women's lounge featured murals of jungle animals done in carved linoleum.

Recalling the Viennese origins of some early Art Deco, Joseph Urban's wallpaper design for the dining room of the Central Park Casino (ca. 1930) in New York presented a bouquet of stylized floral patterns. The casino was demolished in 1936.

White walls captured the public's imagination in the 1930s: they filmed well for black-and-white movies and made dramatic backdrops for the likes of Fred Astaire and Greta Garbo. Wallpapers were generally avoided as unstylish, certainly lacking the panache of plain, painted walls.

But before such sleek surfaces came into vogue, there was color and lots of it. "Color, of course, runs riot in the modern scheme of things," proclaimed *Good Furniture* magazine in 1926, "yet many of the combinations are not half as bizarre as they sound. Brilliant blue, a vibrant magenta, or a vivid purple become merely rich and striking when toned

down with surroundings of dull silver." For a 1928 exhibition Donald Deskey padded the walls in a man's smoking room with cork: "curious, exceedingly interesting cork walls in shades of brown."

Public spaces in public buildings at times could "run riot," with rich patinas of color unifying disparate decorative elements. Painted walls there often meant murals, as a great new age of public art began, culminating in the WPA projects of the 1930s. Exotic and classical allusions filled movie theater side walls, while in skyscrapers modern laborers marched around their machines and streamlined vessels sailed into the future

The arts and crafts production coming almost exclusively from the Wiener Werkstätte brings us the dream flowers of this fairytale world: apparitions resembling rare orchids, artificially grown, having no function....
—Hans Tietze, "Die Wiener Werkstätte," 1920

FLOORS

One of the most popular and expressive floor materials of the Art Deco period was terrazzo, a composite made by embedding small colored stones in concrete and then polishing the surface. Terrazzo artisans produced floor patterns in a multitude of lustrous tones and dynamic shapes from geometric sunbursts to native American motifs. Allen True's floors for the interior spaces of Hoover Dam (1936), for example, wrapped machine-age metaphors in patterns reminiscent of Indian sand paintings. The sculptural monument adjacent to the dam included a terrazzo floor with a celestial map showing the precise astronomical time the dam was dedicated: 8:56 P.M., September 30, 1935.

Marble and tile, including tile mosaics, also were widely used. In bathrooms small, white tiles in hexagonal and other shapes became ubiquitous. Linoleum, invented in 1863, came into its own as a popular floor covering in the 1920s and especially in the cost-conscious Depression years. In battleship gray or polychromatic, geometric patterns, printed and inlaid linoleum spread its glossy hues throughout many houses—not just in kitchens but in foyers, living areas, and bedrooms as well.

Visitors to one Art Deo apartment house in the Bronx, New York, were greeted by this striking terrazzo floor in hues of pumpkin, brown, and gold. The building (1936, Jules Kabat for Horace Ginsbern) became known as the "Fish" apartments because of its colorful exterior mosaic.

Floor coverings and hangings are at least as much a part of the house as the plaster on the walls or the tiles on the roof.
—Frank Lloyd Wright, *Ausgeführte Bauten und Entwürfe von Frank Lloyd Wright*, 1910

Art Deco shone in elevator doors, such as the Niagara Mohawk Building (1932, Bley and Lyman) in Syracuse, New York (above), with its plant and machine forms, and the Chrysler Building (1930), whose panels are veneers of inlaid wood (opposite).

Architects and engineers strove for innovations in mechanical systems in the interwar decades. Building on earlier air-circulation and heating inventions, the art of air conditioning advanced from forced natural air cooling—the use of large fans to pull cool exterior air through a building's ventilation system—to the first use of air conditioning on a par with today's.

Art Deco found its way into the outward surfaces of many building systems as well—from sculpted ventilation grilles, like the geometric bronze gates designed by René Paul Chambellan for the lobby of New York's Chanin Building (1929), to water fountains and bathroom fixtures, like the ones produced by Jacques Delamarre for the Chanin Building's executive bathroom suite, to the multitude of exquisite Art Deco elevator doors and even elevator cabs that can be found in skyscrapers and other buildings of the period worldwide.

FINISHING TOUCHES

Lo! Rectilinear the Cupboard climbs

(Always politely moving with the Times).

Step upon step ascending to its Climax,

Within its sheath of Aluminum Plymax.

—Excerpt from poem by Michael Dugdale,
Architectural Review, March 1932

Raymond Loewy and Lee Simonson designed
this prototypical industrial designer's office for the
1934 Contemporary American Industrial Design
exhibition at the Metropolitan Museum of Art.
With its shining chrome and sleek lines, it captured
the essence of streamlining.

Why not skyscraper furniture? After all, space is as much at a premium within the home as it is outside of it.
—Paul T. Frankl,
House and Garden,
February 1927

From the 1920s came Joseph Urban's terraced table (below) and Abel Faidy's whimsical skyscraper chair for a penthouse (opposite).

In France the preeminent master of early Art Deco furniture design was Emile-Jacques Ruhlmann, a master craftsman whose works occupied an entire pavilion at the 1925 Paris exposition. Ruhlmann's delicate pieces used rare and exotic materials. Other important French furniture designers included Louis Süe and André Mare, Jean Dunand, Pierre Chareau, and Edgar Brandt.

In America Deco furniture was influenced by a number of European expatriates, especially Paul T. Frankl and Joseph Urban (from Austria) and Kem Weber (from Germany). Frankl's designs for terraced bookcases mimicked the silhouettes of skyscrapers. Another outstanding figure in the late

1920s was Donald Deskey, who produced hundreds of modernistic designs using new industrial materials such as Bakelite and stainless steel. While admiring radical modernism, Deskey refused to disavow expressive and ornamental styling. The same could be said for the work of a number of important architects—Eliel Saarinen, Ely Jacques Kahn, and Ralph T. Walker—who designed thirteen room ensembles for a 1929 exhibition at the Metropolitan Museum of Art entitled The Architect and the Industrial Arts.

In the 1930s furniture was affected as much by the streamlining vogue as any other manufactured product. The Simmons Company hired Norman Bel Geddes to design bedroom furniture, and Russel Wright was retained by Heywood-Wakefield. One of the most ubiquitous manifestations of Art Deco appeared in radio cabinetry. Almost all the major brand-name radios— Zenith, RCA, Philco, and dozens of others—were offered in highly modernistic cabinetwork, for both floor and tableside listening.

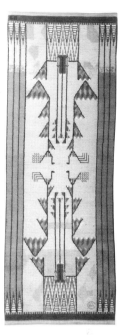

Eliel and Loja Saarinen's Rug No. 2 (1928) recalls native motifs (above), while a French textile used curves and zigzags (opposite). In a Denver Zephyr lounge car (pages 58–59), curves were counterbalanced with angular patterns.

Art Deco textiles were generated in France by major designers such as Robert Mallet-Stevens, studios such as Paul Poiret's Atelier Martine, and department stores. In Britain the most prominent designers were E. Mc-Knight Kauffer and the American expatriate Marion Dorn; both were commissioned in 1927 to design carpets for Wilton. Textiles varied from abstract geometric forms to floral patterns and representational visions such as skyscraper skylines. Carpet patterns tended to be more abstract; textiles for other products—tablecloths, wall hangings, clothing fabrics—used representational motifs as well as abstract patterns.

American textile mills were leery at first about modernistic "fads," but by the late 1920s the major department stores were able to persuade them that Art Deco carpets and fabrics were a winning proposition. Gifted textile designers such as Ruth Reeves had already begun to render modernistic themes in their woven and printed work—some of which had been exhibited in galleries by the late 1920s—and when up-and-coming interior designers such as Donald Deskey created their own custom Art Deco textile designs, the manufacturers' conversion was complete.

Draperies in Deco interiors were every bit as likely to display the archetypal motifs of the period as any other surface. These "blonde white" novelty curtains were designed by Prou, an interior design firm in Paris.

The usual house of today is rigid. The House of Tomorrow is flexible. At one moment, with venetian blinds raised and the curtains drawn back, one feels as though he were out of doors, an exhilarating and unusual sensation.
—Home and Furnishings: A Century of Progress, 1934

The draperies used in Art Deco interiors varied little in most respects from earlier arrangements of a classical or classicizing kind, although the ornamental patterns sometimes printed on the draperies could be quite distinctive.

What was striking in the 1930s, however, was the unabashed revival of Venetian blinds as a window amenity with visually expressive possibilities. Specifically, with the advent of streamlining the linear horizontality of Venetian blinds provided an accent for modernistic surroundings. In the Astaire and Rogers film *The Gay Divorcée* (1934), the dance to Cole Porter's "Night and Day" took place on a seaside terrace with windows fitted with Venetian blinds, which cast moody shadows across the dance floor. For a moment the camera tracked the dancing couple from the outside of the terrace looking in, through the slats of the blinds. That same year a promotional brochure for George Fred Keck's House of Tomorrow at the 1933–34 Century of Progress Exposition proclaimed, "By using venetian blinds, roller shades and curtains ... the light through these glass walls can be controlled from absolute darkness to as full light as nature affords."

LIGHTING AND LAMPS

Art Deco left its touch on almost every form of lighting: table lamps, floor lamps, chandeliers, and wall fixtures. Jean Perzel and other French lamp designers produced strikingly modernistic fixtures in the 1920s.

One of the most important designers was Walter von Nessen, a German expatriate known for boldly modernistic fixtures. Donald Deskey and industrial designers such as Walter Dorwin Teague also turned their talents to lighting. Department stores and manufacturers brought out hundreds of lines of modernistic lighting in the 1920s and 1930s, much of it inspired by the well-publicized creations of the big-name designers.

One of the most typical and evocative Art Deco lighting fixtures was the torchère, a floor lamp with an upturned shade (or terraced shades) that cast indirect lighting on the ceiling. The Frankart boudoir lamp, a small table fixture created by Arthur von Frankenberg, used nudes to hold up illuminated cylinders or globes. Through such fixtures the spirit of the 1925 Paris exposition was diffused to the point of pervasiveness in the years between the world wars. Here was exotica—or perhaps just a dose of escapist whimsy—for everyman and everywoman.

A Walter von Nessen torchère (ca. 1928) featured expressive ribbing in brushed chrome over brass.

A stairway in the Kalamazoo, Michigan, city hall (1930, Weary and Alford) is graced with a cast-aluminum light.

DECO DESIGN

Americans competed with European artisans to produce fine Deco objects such as the crystal designed for Steuben Glass by Sidney Waugh, including his Gazelle Bowl of 1935.

Chromium-plated and enameled steel, cast aluminum, vinyl, and rubber were combined in this classic Electrolux vacuum cleaner of 1937, designed by Lurelle Guild.

From the most expensive silver by Jean Puiforcat and glasswork by René Lalique to everyday Fiesta Ware ceramics and Fada radios, Art Deco left its mark on luxuries as well as mass-produced objects.

Influenced by the ideals of the earlier Wiener Werkstätte and Deutsche Werkbund as well as the Bauhaus, various designers preached the reconciliation of art, industry, and merchandising and offered industrial clients complete restylings. Their skill and promotional flair were undeniable. By the early 1930s Raymond Loewy, Norman Bel Geddes, Walter Dorwin Teague, Henry Dreyfuss, and Gilbert Rohde were names to conjure with. Most became missionaries for streamlining; Bel Geddes's 1932 book, *Horizons*, was a manifesto.

By the late 1930s their look-of-speed streamlining appeared in almost every conceivable object, from Teague's new camera designs for Kodak to Dreyfuss's Thermos pitchers to Loewy's chrome pencil sharpeners. Through thousands of products, Art Deco and streamlining came to permeate the marketplace, the office, and the home.

Sidney Waugh

While radical modernists boasted that their chaste, abstract creations heralded a new "International Style," the world popularity of Art Deco was far greater in the years between the wars. With the exception of free-standing houses (in which more traditional styling predominated), Art Deco had a major impact on almost the entire range of buildings and structures in the industrialized world.

Some of the new streamlined aircraft deposited their passengers in streamlined airports. Among the more important examples was the Pan American Seaplane Base in Miami (1932, Delano and Aldrich).

HOUSES AND HOTELS

Although Art Deco was an exception when it came to the detached single-family house, the exceptions were striking—such as the streamlined Butler house (1936, Kraetsch and Kraetsch) in Des Moines, Iowa.

At the same time that radical modernists such as Le Corbusier were designing truly avant-garde houses for a handful of daring (and wealthy) clients, toned-down versions of modern residences emerged in Europe from the studios of architects such as Robert Mallet-Stevens. In residential districts across America, from Beverly Hills to Miami Beach, exotic hybrid houses fused Deco with traditional residential forms.

Art Deco was more prominent in apartment buildings and hotels. Because of the Depression, thousands of low-rise and mid-rise apartments—especially FHA-supported garden apartment complexes—predominated in the United States by the mid-1930s.

Art Deco hotels ran the gamut from palatial buildings such as New York's Waldorf-Astoria (1931, Schultze and Weaver) to mid-size luxury resorts such as Britain's Midland Hotel (1934, Oliver Hill) to Miami Beach's myriad low-rise hotels of the late 1930s and early 1940s. The hotel's great new competitor—the motel—was also affected by Art Deco. Designed for motor-age convenience, motels such as the Coral Court near St. Louis (1941, Adolph L. Struebig) are significant components of the Deco legacy.

Smooth surfaces, sharp edges, clean curves, polished materials, right angles; clarity and order. Such is the logical and geometric house of tomorrow.
—Robert Mallet-Stevens, *Le Bulletin de la vie artistique,* 1924

Loretta Young bedded
down in Art Deco
comfort in the 1928 film
The Magnificent Flirt.

Large and imposing
Art Deco apartments
appeared in the late
1920s and 1930s.

The Kennedy-Warren
(1931, Joseph Younger)
remains a landmark in
Washington, D.C.

GREENBELT TOWNS

Completed in 1937, Greenbelt is one of the most fully realized examples of Art Deco architecture synthesized with conservationist landscape ideals. Its school features a series of bas reliefs depicting portions of the preamble to the U.S. Constitution.

One of the great design challenges carried over from the nineteenth century was the attempt to harmonize industrial-age urbanism with the landscape. Given the impact of the automobile, the challenge became more urgent. From the British Victorian theorist Ebenezer Howard had come the vision of the garden city: the planned, low-density suburb. Planning reformers such as Clarence Stein, Catherine Bauer, and Rexford Guy Tugwell sought to bring these ideals to fruition in the twentieth century. The turn-of-the-century City Beautiful movement also had a lingering influence. Frank Lloyd Wright's desire to build organic architecture in harmony with the landscape combined with his enthusiasm for the automobile in

his vision of a Broadacre City linked by thrilling motor parkways.

A brief New Deal experiment combined a number of these principles. Under the Greenbelt Towns program, three suburban model towns were constructed: Greenbelt (in Maryland), Greendale (in Wisconsin), and Greenhills (in Ohio). In Greenbelt streamlined architecture was placed in a setting of verdant beauty. Residential housing blocks were set amid wooded pathways, and pedestrian underpasses were constructed to protect children from traffic.

As Art Deco sought to mediate between extremes of design, the garden city was the realization of perennial desires for a golden mean between nature and civilization.

Let us keep
ourselves,
our community,
our city government,
our ideals,
as clean as our new,
windswept roofs.
—Mary E. Van Cleave,
"We Pioneers,"
The Greenbelt
Cooperator, 1937

A 1931 mailbox at
Northwestern Bell in
Minneapolis (above)
resembles a skyscraper,
like those at Rockefeller
Center (opposite).

Crammed on
the narrow island
the million-
windowed buildings
will jut glittering,
pyramid on pyramid
like the white
cloud-head above
a thunderstorm.
—John Dos Passos, *Man-*
hattan Transfer, 1925

SKYSCRAPERS

Nothing epitomized Art Deco more than the greatest of the tall office buildings: skyscrapers. As an icon of progress the skyscraper reawakened the imagery of ancient archetypes; their setback terracing was strangely evocative of Babylonian ziggurats and Aztec pyramids. Architectural renderer Hugh Ferriss captured this eeriness in his 1929 book, *The Metropolis of Tomorrow.* Some writers made the theme explicit; John Dos Passos, in *Manhattan Transfer* (1925) invoked the imagery of ancient monuments and then tried to visualize the Manhattan of the future.

Art Deco skyscrapers strongly integrated ornament with form and structure, and the ornamentation was often as elaborate in the upper setback stories and crown—consider the extravagant stainless-steel spire of the Chrysler Building (1930)—as in the lower stories. Lobbies and public spaces could be extremely elegant.

New York was the leader in Deco skyscrapers, but even in smaller cities the presence of a "skyscraper" (however diminutive compared to the prodigies of Gotham City) became an imperative status symbol—provided that the economy could make such a venture possible after 1929.

INDUSTRIAL BUILDINGS

However prosaic the task of designing industrial buildings and factories might appear, designers and architects took the challenge seriously in the interwar decades. This was not a new trend—architects had found inspiration for years in the challenge of designing a model workplace. But in an age when industrial designers were increasingly figures of celebrity, the prestige of designing industrial buildings increased. Norman Bel Geddes featured visions of clean and utopian factories in his book *Horizons* (1932). Prominent architects such as Albert Kahn made a specialty of efficient factories, and even world-renowned architects such as Frank Lloyd Wright sought industrial commissions. Wright's designs for the Johnson Wax Administration Building (1936) and Research Tower (1944) are regarded as masterworks in the genre of streamlined architecture.

Streamlining was applied to a number of important industrial buildings in the 1930s, from the spectacular Coca Cola Bottling Plant in Los Angeles (1936, Robert Derrah), with its ocean-liner detailing, to Sir Giles Gilbert Scott's design for London's Battersea Power Station (1934), a fusion of modernized classicism with Art Deco detailing.

The award-winning Hecht Company Warehouse (1937, Abbott, Merkt) in Washington, D.C., was noted for its use of glass block. Across town, Paul Philippe Cret's Central Heating and Refrigeration Plant (1934) sports bas-relief sculpted panels depicting workers and machines.

Can a first-rate product be manufactured in a third-rate plant? It is no longer advisable to set up a standardized structure, relying on company architects to adapt it to company needs.
—Norman Bel Geddes, *Horizons,* 1932

While the 1920s were the golden age of the picture palace, the impact of Art Deco was not seen until the final years of the building boom. The incomparable Radio City Music Hall (1932) was a key part of the Rockefeller Center complex; its magnificent Deco interior was designed by Edward Durell Stone and Donald Deskey.

The Depression brought the picture palace era to an end; after that, the size of theaters was dramatically downscaled. But thousands of smaller Art Deco theaters were built in the 1930s, many designed by nationally renowned architects, among them John Eberson and Thomas Lamb. In Great Britain an array of Deco and streamlined cinemas came from architects such as E. Wamsley Lewis, Harry Weedon, and Iles, Leathart and Grainger.

Art Deco affected other entertainment structures as well, from Playland (1927, Walker and Gillette) in Rye, New York, to Hollywood's enormous streamlined Pan-Pacific Auditorium (1935, Wurdeman and Becket)—ignominiously razed in the 1980s.

One of the most stunning Deco movie theaters is the Paramount (1931, Timothy Pflueger) in Oakland, California, whose elaborate auditorium (opposite) recalls the 1925 Paris exposition. Theatrical motifs in the lobby include a bevy of golden dancers (above).

The 1939 New York World's Fair's famous architectural symbols, the geometric Trylon and Perisphere, were designed by architects Wallace Harrison and J. André Fouilhoux. Inside the Perisphere, industrial designer Henry Dreyfuss created a diorama called Democracity.

Designers at the 1939 New York World's Fair

Alvar Aalto

Norman Bel Geddes

Henry Dreyfuss

J. André Fouilhoux

Wallace Harrison

Albert Kahn

Raymond Loewy

Gilbert Rohde

Skidmore and Owings

Walter Dorwin Teague

Russel Wright

After the 1925 Paris exposition a series of world's fairs helped spread Art Deco. From France again came the 1931 Exposition Coloniale Internationale de Paris and the 1937 Exposition Internationale des Arts et Techniques dans la Vie Moderne.

The first American fair to trumpet Deco was the 1933 Century of Progress Exposition celebrating Chicago's centenary. Architect Raymond Hood oversaw the board of design. The buildings and exhibits emphasized industrial technology and advanced building materials. Amazingly, in the midst of the Depression the fair made money.

Encouraged, in 1939 San Francisco hosted the Golden Gate International Exposition and New York opened its own world's fair. The San Francisco exposition, built on the specially created Treasure Island, featured buildings with ornate zigzag terracing and opulent ornamentation. The elaborate Elephant Towers by Blackwell and Weihe were among the most prominent examples. The New York World's Fair, by contrast, was given over to streamlining and visions of the World of Tomorrow; in the General Motors pavilion a visionary Futurama depicted the urban world of 1960.

Art Deco had an overwhelming impact on retail architecture, especially in the United States. It was embraced by the largest and most prominent retail concerns: the department stores. Their architecture, interior design, furnishings, and advertising reflected the style, from stores in the upper stratum like Bloomingdale's (1930) in New York and Bullock's (1928) in Los Angeles to the chain stores like Sears, Kress, and Woolworth.

What was good for the chains was also good for mom-and-pop concerns. Throughout the 1930s merchants built Art Deco and streamlined stores or else remodeled older ones to make them appear modernistic, complete with neon or porcelain enamel signs. Entire retail districts were influenced by Art Deco: the Miracle Mile in Los Angeles was one of the most ambitious.

New retail strategies generated new building types—supermarkets, motor-age shopping centers, and restaurant chains, especially drive-ins and hamburger stands—that quickly adopted Art Deco and streamlining. Diners and prefabricated (or movable) buildings produced by hamburger chains like White Towers brought the spirit of Jazz Age living to the everyday lunch counter.

One of the most distinctive Art Deco drive-ins was Herbert's (1938, Wayne McAllister) in Los Angeles. Along with diners, which were custom-designed and mass-manufactured widely by the 1930s, such fast-food outlets helped change the era's eating habits.

One compact shopping center designed to serve the needs of 50,000 persons! That is the plan behind the Silver Spring Shopping Center. . . . Everything from toothpicks to radios can be purchased within one area and with one parking.
—The Washington Post, October 27, 1938

Practicing "modernized classicism," Bertram G. Goodhue produced Nebraska's 1932 capitol (above) and the 1926 Los Angeles Public Library (opposite).

The Moderne traditionalized, the Traditional modernized.
—*The Federal Architect*, 1930

Art Deco's mediational role—its function as a middle range between conservative and radical design—is especially apparent in municipal and public buildings. A great many architects were striving for a reasonable compromise that would salute both the past and the future while making a strong contemporary statement.

This goal had particular resonance for public officials. From town halls to capitols, the compromise formula was typically a synthesis of Greco-Roman classicism with modernist simplification of form—to which the ornamental language of the 1925 Paris exposition as well as 1930s streamlining were added to energize the composition.

From Franklin D. Roosevelt's Washington, commissions for New Deal public works projects radiated outward across America. Many of the buildings that resulted were stunning examples of the modernized classical version of Art Deco: courthouses, post offices, schools, and auditoriums. This version of Art Deco was internationally influential: many of the buildings at the Paris exposition of 1937 could be said to have represented a traditionalized moderne and a modernized traditional.

The apotheosis of locomotive design coincided with the last great period of railroad station design. Perhaps the ultimate Art Deco depot was the Cincinnati Union Terminal (1933, Fellheimer and Wagner).

The great theme-givers for aerodynamic streamlining were the airplane and the train. In the late 1920s aeronautical design began to emphasize sleek and cohesive contours—for instance, the Lockheed Sirius of 1929 and the Douglas DC-series and especially the DC-3 of 1935–36. Flying was given an air of romantic luxury with the introduction of "flying boats," the huge Clipper seaplanes.

Industrial designers began to apply the same principles to the railroad; the first streamlined trains—the Burlington Zephyr and the Milwaukee Road's Hiawatha—hit the rails in 1934. Industrial designers vied to create the most impressive-looking locomotives; Raymond Loewy's s-1 (1937–39) and Henry Dreyfuss's 20th-Century Limited (1938) were the clear front-runners.

Deco Depots

Union Passenger
  Terminal (1939),
  Los Angeles
Union Station,
  Omaha (1929)
30th Street Station,
  Philadelphia (1929)
Union Depot,
  Tulsa (1931)

Gulf Oil was notable for its ornate Art Deco service stations, among them this 1936 example in Pittsburgh. The same year Texaco commissioned Walter Dorwin Teague to design a range of streamlined gas station prototypes.

Many people could not afford a car in the Depression—but the emergence of Greyhound Lines in the United States, with its intercontinental bus network, made long-distance motor-age transport available to millions at low-budget prices. Greyhound commissioned Raymond Loewy to update its coach design, and the result was the streamlined Greyhound Super Coach (1935).

America's road system was expanded tremendously in the 1920s and 1930s. An ambitious network of roadways and parkways such as Connecticut's Merritt Parkway (1940) sported features (especially bridges) influenced by Art Deco. Deco was also on display in the bridges of the Pennsylvania Turnpike (1941). Scores of other Art Deco bridges were constructed in the 1930s, many of them as public works projects.

New building types emerged for the motor age—principally the gasoline station and the bus terminal—and Art Deco fit them well. A handful of firms began designing streamlined bus terminals for Greyhound. The pièce de résistance was the "super terminal" in Washington, D.C. (1940, Wischmeyer, Arrasmith and Elswick)—dubbed the Grand Central of the Motor Bus World.

He fancied that this was veritably the temple of a new divinity, the God of Speed. Of its adherents it demanded... a belief that Going Somewhere, Going Quickly, Going Often, were in themselves holy....
—Sinclair Lewis, *Dodsworth,* 1929

SOURCES OF INFORMATION

**Art Deco Society
of Boston**
1 Murdock Terrace
Brighton, Mass. 02135

**Art Deco Society
of California**
100 Bush Street
Suite 511
San Francisco, Calif.
94104

**Art Deco Society
of New York**
385 Fifth Avenue
Suite 501
New York, N.Y. 10016

**Art Deco Society
of Washington**
P.O. Box 11090
Washington, D.C. 20008

Art Deco Trust
P.O. Box 248
Napier, New Zealand

**Canadian
Art Deco Society**
101–1080 Barclay Street
Vancouver, B.C., V6E
1G7 Canada

**Detroit Area
Art Deco Society**
P.O. Box 1393
Royal Oak, Mich. 48068

**Kansas City
Art Deco Society**
9104 Fontana
Prairie Village, Kans.
66207

**Los Angeles
Conservancy**
433 South Spring Street
Suite 124
Los Angeles, Calif.
90013

**Miami Design
Preservation League**
P.O. Bin L
Miami Beach, Fla. 33119

**Society for
Commercial Archeology**
National Museum of
American History
Room 5010
Washington, D.C. 20560

**Society of
Architectural Historians**
1232 Pine Street
Philadelphia, Pa.
19107–5944

**The Twentieth
Century Society**
58 Crescent Lane
London, SW4 9PV
England

**Vernacular
Architecture Forum**
109 Brandon Road
Baltimore, Md. 21212

SITES TO VISIT

*See additional places
cited in the text.*

**Adams Building, Library
of Congress (1939)**
Washington, D.C.

Art Museum (1932)
Seattle, Wash.

Coit Tower (1933)
San Francisco, Calif.

**Daily Express Building
(1931)**
London, England

Fair Park (1936)
Dallas, Tex.

**Folger Shakespeare
Library (1932)**
Washington, D.C.

**450 Sutter Medical
Building (1928)**
San Francisco, Calif.

Hollywood Bowl (1940)
Hollywood, Calif.

**House of Tomorrow
(1933)**
Indiana Dunes National
Lakeshore, Ind.

Louisiana Capitol (1931)
Baton Rouge, La.

Marine Building (1930)
Vancouver, B.C.

**Municipal Auditorium
(1933)**
Kansas City, Mo.

**Netherland Plaza Hotel
(1930)**
Cincinnati, Ohio

**New England Telephone
and Telegraph (1930)**
Boston, Mass.

**Ocean Drive
and Collins Avenue**
Miami Beach, Fla.

**Palmolive (Playboy)
Building (1927)**
Chicago, Ill.

**Paramount Theater
(1929)**
Aurora, Ill.

**Ramsey County
Courthouse–St. Paul
City Hall (1931)**
St. Paul, Minn.

St. James Church (1937)
Vancouver, B.C.

**Union Trust (Guardian)
Building (1928)**
Detroit, Mich.

**WCAU Radio Station
(1931)**
Philadelphia, Pa.

**Will Rogers High School
(1938)**
Tulsa, Okla.

RECOMMENDED READING

Arwas, Victor. *Art Deco*. New York: Abrams, 1980.

Bush, Donald J. *The Streamlined Decade*. New York: Braziller, 1975.

Capitman, Barbara. *Deco Delights*. New York: Dutton, 1988.

Capitman, Barbara, Michael D. Kinerk, and Dennis W. Wilhelm. *Rediscovering Art Deco U.S.A.: A Nationwide Tour of Architectural Delights*. New York: Viking Studio Books, 1994.

Duncan, Alastair. *American Art Deco*. New York: Abrams, 1986.

Gutman, Richard J. S., and Elliott Kaufman. *American Diner*. New York: Harper and Row, 1979.

Hillier, Bevis. *Art Deco*. London: Dutton Studio Vista, 1968.

————. *The World of Art Deco*. New York: Dutton, 1971.

Krinsky, Carol Herselle. *Rockefeller Center*. New York: Oxford University Press, 1978.

Liebs, Chester H. *Main Street to Miracle Mile: American Roadside Architecture*. Boston: Little, Brown, 1985.

Mandelbaum, Howard, and Eric Myers. *Screen Deco*. New York: St. Martin's, 1985.

Meikle, Jeffrey. *Twentieth-Century Limited: Industrial Design in America, 1925–1939*. Philadelphia: Temple University Press, 1979.

Robinson, Cervin, and Rosemarie Haag Bletter. *Skyscraper Style: Art Deco New York*. New York: Oxford University Press, 1975.

Striner, Richard. "Art Deco: Polemics and Synthesis," *Winterthur Portfolio* 25, no. 1 (Spring 1990): 21–34.

Wilson, Richard Guy, Dianne H. Pilgrim, and Dickran Tashjian. *The Machine Age in America, 1918–1941*. New York: Abrams, 1986.

Wirz, Hans, and Richard Striner. *Washington Deco: Art Deco Design in the Nation's Capital*. Washington, D.C.: Smithsonian Institution Press, 1984.

Endpapers: Art Deco
Shell carpet reproduc-
tion, Bloomsburg
Carpet Industries

Page 1: Air-King radio
(1930, Harold van
Doren and J. G. Rideout)
Page 2: Chrysler
Building (1930,
William Van Alen)
Page 5: Isamu Noguchi
working on a plaque
for the Associated Press
Building at Rockefeller
Center in 1939

Produced by
Archetype Press, Inc.
Project Director:
Diane Maddex
Art Director:
Robert L. Wiser

Copyright © 1994 Archetype Press, Inc., and Abbeville
Press. Compilation—including selection, placement,
and order of text and images—© 1994 Archetype
Press, Inc., and Abbeville Press. Text © 1994 Richard
Striner. All rights reserved under international
copyright conventions. No part of this book may be
reproduced or utilized in any form or by any means,
electronic or mechanical, including photocopying,
recording, or by any information storage and retrieval
system, without permission in writing from the
publisher. Inquiries should be addressed to Abbeville
Publishing Group, 488 Madison Avenue, New York,
N.Y. 10022. Printed and bound in China.

First edition, second printing

Library of Congress Cataloging-in-Publication Data
Striner, Richard
Art deco / Richard Striner.
    p.   cm. — (Stylebooks)
"An Archetype Press book."
Includes bibliographical references.
ISBN 1-55859-824-3
1. Art deco. I. Title. II. Series.
N6494.A7S76 1994
724'.6–dc20   94-18571

CREDITS

Barnes Communications, courtesy Kizette Foxhall: 21

Bison Archives: 16–17, 72

Bloomsburg Carpet Industries: endpapers

Robert Bonfils: 26

Steven Brooke: jacket source

Brooklyn Museum: 1 (no. 85.9, Walter Foundation), 66 (no. 86.15, gift of Fifty-50)

Chevron: 90–91 (Johnston and Johnston)

Chicago Historical Society: Hedrich-Blessing Collection, 47 (HB-04382 N), 70–71 (HB 04045 S); Decorative and Industrial Arts Department Collection, 57 (no. 1977.191.2e)

Columbia University, Butler Rare Book and Manuscript Library, Joseph Urban Papers: 48–49, 56

Cooper-Hewitt Museum: 24 (gift of Mrs. Hugh Ferriss, no. 1969-137-4); Bonney Collection, 13, 18, 19, 36, 61, 63

Corning Museum of Glass, gift of Mr. and Mrs. John K. Olsen: 67

Cranbrook Academy of Art Museum: 60

Culver Pictures: 10

Historic American Buildings Survey: 28, 35, 38, 42, 43, 68, 74–75, 80, 81

© Randy Juster: 39, 50, 52, 53, 64, 76

Library of Congress: 40, 44, 73, 78, 83, 88–89

Los Angeles Public Library, History Department: 87

Metropolitan Museum of Art: 55

Natural History Museum of Los Angeles County, Seaver Center for Western History Research: 84

Nebraska State Historical Society: 86

Christian Poite: 27

© Cervin Robinson: 2

© The Rockefeller Group: 77

Roger-Viollet: 22

Turner Entertainment Company, © 1938. All rights reserved; courtesy Jerry Ohlinger's Movie Material Store: 8

Underwood Photo Archives: 33, 58–59; courtesy Isamu Noguchi Foundation, 5

Yale University Art Gallery, Enoch Vine Stoddard and Marie-Antoinette Slade Funds: 65